EMPLOYEE
RETENTION
Rules!

EMPLOYEE RETENTION Rules!

52 ways to reduce employee turnover

HAROLD C. LLOYD

illustrated by STEVE HICKNER

BRIGANTINE MEDIA

Illustrations by Steve Hickner

Brigantine Media
211 North Avenue, St. Johnsbury, Vermont 05819
802-751-8802 | Fax: 802-751-8804
neil@brigantinemedia.com
www.brigantinemedia.com

www.therulesbooks.com

ISBN 978-1-938406-6-9-0

The Rules

The Rules

Introduction

Fact: Replacing a minimum-wage-earning employee costs the average retail business about $3,500 every time it happens.

On average, a retail business replaces 59 percent of its workforce every year. So if you have 100 employees, turnover costs you $206,500 every year. If you have 1,000 employees, that's more than $2 million in employee turnover costs! Those numbers can destroy a bottom line.

Companies can't afford this "average" level of employee turnover. It's time to learn how to improve your employee retention rate.

In this book, I've distilled 52 rules for retaining your employees. It comes down to five key responsibilities of management. When a company handles these five responsibilities really well, employees stay with the company longer.

Management needs to provide employees with:

- thorough **orientation** to the job at the start and continued opportunities to learn

- consistent **communication** every day

- respectful **discipline** and fair treatment when they make mistakes

- sincere **recognition** when they do something exceptional

- annual **performance evaluations** that offer a clear path to future professional growth

I am so sure of the importance of these principles for reducing turnover that I include them in every seminar I give on employee retention. I ask participants to rate their stores on these five management responsibilities. They score each category 1 to 20, for a possible total score of 100.

I'm sorry to report that in the retail industry, the average score is a woeful 44.

This low score provides an answer to the question, "Why don't people want to work in retail?" My observation is, "Why would they? We're giving them less than half (44%) of what keeps employees in their jobs!"

What's your score? Have your managers rate their performance on executing these five management responsibilities:

Orientation (first thirty days)   1 – 20 _____

Communication (up and down)   1 – 20 _____

Discipline (fair and consistent)   1 – 20 _____

Recognition (daily, annually)   1 – 20 _____

Performance Evaluations (annual   1 – 20 _____
    plan to succeed)

Total _____

This is your store's Employee Retention score. How does it stack up against others? The great companies score at least 80. The really good ones score 65 or more. Just like in school, less than a 65 should be considered a failing grade—and if your score is less than 65, you're probably complaining about not being able to find good help.

In this book, we're adding one more management responsibility: Recruiting/Hiring. That happens before the employee is on board, but it has great impact on your rate of employee retention. If you're not recruiting and hiring the right people for the jobs, they are destined to leave your company quickly.

Read this book and implement some of its powerful employee retention best practices. Try one rule each week. A year from now, score your store again. When you reach the 80s or even better, the 90s, you'll be able to say *your* **Employee Retention Rules!**

PART ONE

Recruiting and Hiring

**Always
recruit.
Always!**

If you are like most retailers, you are always in need of good employees. But are you always in recruitment mode?

I advocate a 24/7 recruiting effort. Even when your company is at full employment, there are probably a few current employees who aren't performing as you would like. Recruiting the best employees possible is the ultimate goal. Continue recruiting until that goal is met.

Sure, there are plenty of recruiting websites like Monster, LinkedIn, Snagajob, ZipRecruiter, Indeed, Job.com, and more. But you can't rely on them exclusively to find all the employees you need.

Make sure all your managers have business cards to offer potential employees they might meet in or outside the store. Teach your front-end management where the employment applications are kept and how to administer a brief but insightful preliminary interview and, if applicable, how to direct the candidate to your newly remodeled employment kiosk. Have professionally made signs—not a Sharpie on a shopping bag—that say "Join Our Family!" or "Join the Team!" (*never* "Help Wanted"), and post them strategically in the store. Offer an employee referral bonus to current employees who refer a friend who gets hired. Meet with high school counselors and Chamber of Commerce officials periodically to be at their top of mind when they are trying to help a student or new resident in the community find a job.

Make a positive, professional, and persistent effort to recruit every day.

Find your best sources
for the best recruits.

How do you find job applicants?

People who are looking for jobs come to you from many different sources. Try to identify which sources bring you the best applicants.

On your employment application, ask "How did you hear about us?" or "How did you know about this employment opportunity?" List different possible sources for the applicant to choose from, such as: newspaper ad, online ad, website, friend, LinkedIn, school guidance counselor, window sign, current employee, a mini-application that is stuffed in shopping bags—whatever. The more specifically you describe possible sources, the better.

Once a year, check the sources that generated the most applications. Then check your list of the twenty best employees you brought on board in the past year. Where did they hear about the job opening? Put that information together and you'll know where to find the employees you really want to hire.

It makes sense to invest more money and time in those sources and less on other alternatives. For example, if "a friend who works here" proves to be a strong source of good applicants, institute an Employee Referral Reward program that offers existing employees money if they refer someone who is ultimately hired. You can let employees know about the program in a newsletter or bulletin board post ("$50 Reward for Helping us Find and Hire ..."). Or if a local high school is consistently sending you good applicants, make sure to attend the school's Job Fair and maybe even be a sponsor.

Don't shoot in the dark. Identify the best sources for the best applicants.

Merchandise your employment kiosk.

Take a look at your employment kiosk that occupies prime space at the front of your store. You might find that it's an eyesore rather than an effective recruiting station.

The employment kiosk is often a company's first contact with an applicant. But when it is tucked in between the Rug Doctor display and the 50-pound bags of dog food, it looks like an afterthought. You spend so much effort merchandising your store's products, why not merchandise your job opportunities just as creatively?

Your employment kiosk should be clean, attractive, and easy to navigate. Make sure potential applicants can find your generous job benefits, motivational mission statement, and inspirational employee testimonials posted on the walls of the kiosk. To attract and retain the best employees, you must look your best at the place where the company and the candidate first meet.

Make your employment kiosk area an important stop on your daily store evaluation tour to be sure it always presents a great first impression. And if you don't have a comfortable place for a candidate to complete an application, create one! Put your best foot forward to attract the best candidates when they visit your store.

Dress for success.

Some time ago, a fast-food operator changed its dress code from dorky to hip and stole five employees in one week from a nearby competitor. It's possible the dress code wasn't the only reason for the mass exodus. But the foodservice world took notice that the employee's uniform can be a recruiting and retention tool.

Be careful that your dress code policy isn't tied to outdated personal preferences. If it is, you'll have fewer applicants, more disgruntled employees, and higher turnover. Strike a balance between function and fashion, between professional and generational. More Starbucks and less Burger King.

When selecting the dress code for my retail operations, I developed the Dennis Rodman test:

- Does an employee's tattoo(s) impede the employee's performance?

- Do an employee's piercings impede the employee's performance?

- Does a specific hair color or style keep an employee from doing the job?

- What part of the dress code can employees choose for themselves?

I did not let my preferences dictate dress code decisions if the employee's personal style did not have a negative effect on his ability to do the job.

Of course you must have high standards and consistency. But let employees be comfortable and uniquely themselves. Then watch your dress code attract and keep good employees.

Conduct reference checks and do background screening.

In employment cases, this is the law of the land: "If you could have known, you should have known." Employers can be held legally responsible for harmful acts employees commit if the employers acted carelessly when hiring and retaining associates.

Always, always, *always* do reference checks. Make sure you verify prior employment and conduct professional, third party background screening for all new hires.

I used to think that if a company verified the last three jobs an applicant held, that was sufficient. Most prior employers give some limited details on applicants with enough information to help a company make hiring decisions.

But I realize now that isn't thorough at all. Today, every company needs to conduct third-party background screening by certified professionals.

An extra ten minutes on the phone to verify previous employment and an additional thirty dollars spent on a top-shelf background screening service is a small investment to make if it helps steer you away from hiring a liar, thief, addict, arsonist, or pedophile. Eventually, you'll end up terminating those employees. But until you do, they can cost you a fortune. This small investment of time and money on the front end of the hiring process can extend your employee retention at the other.

I'm always amazed when a retailer tells me he stopped doing reference checks or background screening, not necessarily because of the expense, but because it shrunk the applicant pool. How's that for absurd logic?

What you don't know about your new hires can and will hurt you.

Conduct three interviews before making an offer.

There are three components to a thorough hiring process—a strong job application, a thorough background investigation, and three positive interviews. All these components are of equal importance and value. All must be favorable to offer the applicant a job.

Who conducts the three interviews?

ONE

The first interview for any job candidate should be conducted by a human resources representative. This person knows employment law and conducts a screening of every applicant. The HR rep is there to "thin the herd" of job applicants who should not be considered further.

TWO

The second interview should be with the store management representative. That person should determine if the candidate will fill the store's needs and can assimilate into the store's culture.

THREE

The third interview should be with the department manager who will directly supervise the new employee. Some companies don't involve the department manager in the selection decision, but I think that's a mistake. You want the department manager to "own" the hiring decision. Imagine the difference between a rental car and a car you own. You're unlikely to wash a rental car because you don't own it. Only when the car feels like it's really your own do you care for it properly. Same with employees.

Some companies add a fourth step to the hiring process—inviting two or three employees from the department to interview the applicant before the final decision is made. These co-workers will be the people impacted the most by the new employee. Why not involve them?

Ask effective interview questions.

Conduct each employment interview as if you are going to write an interesting biography about the candidate. Create a list of five or six questions that elicit robust, insightful responses. Use those same questions in every interview so you can compare the responses to them. And keep interviewing a candidate until you find something unique or interesting. You have to find a way to make the best applicants stand out on your mind.

Everyone who interviews employee candidates has a favorite interview question. One of mine is if the applicant has a pet, or maybe a bird feeder. I like to know if they have an interest in taking care of something. If they do, I often find them better at customer relations.

Interviewing is an art and a science. Some people are very good at interviewing, and others aren't. Who were your twenty best new hires in the last year? Check who was in on the interview process. It's easy to track this if each interviewer initials the application after the interview. Then develop a small group of people who are more successful at identifying the best candidates. Let that group do more interviewing in the future.

In my experience, "A" managers will identify "A" candidates. "B" managers will select "C" employees. "C" and "D" managers won't care who they hire. They just want to fill a vacancy.

If at first you don't succeed, try one more time.

Retailers are always trying to get customers back again after they leave and start shopping elsewhere. Some keep lists of customers who haven't shopped with them for a year and send them special offers to encourage them to come back to the store. It can work to remind an old customer to give you another try.

Try this same idea to attract ex-employees back to work with you. And you wouldn't be the first—Disney does it! Here's an excerpt from a letter the Walt Disney World Company sent to previously employed associates (cast members):

> *Dear Former Cast Member:*
>
> *Things haven't been the same since you left. And we want you to know that if the grass out there isn't as green as you hoped it would be, you're always welcome to come home and explore the opportunities that are still available to you with Walt Disney World Co.*

Why give another opportunity to an employee who left the company? Many people would think he should be banished from the premises forever.

But Disney (and others) recognize that the above-average employee should be welcomed back —once. Just think of all the savings in orientation and training expenses. And it's quite possible the rehired associate will become a staunch company advocate because he has seen the other side and has been given a second chance.

A letter, sent six months after an above-average employee has left may be the little push the employee needs to reapply with your company. Give it a try!

PART TWO

Orientation

Be there on Day One!

The store manager should be there on Day One to greet the new employee at the front door. Remember, first impressions count.

Start the employee's first day with a warm greeting from the store manager. Have the manager give the new employee a tour of the store, then spend a bit of time in the office. At the end of the newbie's first shift, the manager and the employee should have a closing conversation.

Of course, a store manager has a lot to do every day. But if our employees are our most important

assets, and if we have a real desire to retain employees, commit 72 minutes to a new employee's first day. That's right, 72 minutes. Here's how it breaks down:

1 A two-minute greeting at the front door. The store manager should set an alarm to remind him to be near the front of the store when the new employee is scheduled to start. Give the employee a big welcome and a "thanks for being on time" (or some immediate coaching if the employee is late).

2 A thirty-minute store tour (see Rule 12) to acquaint the employee with the store and make clear the store's key points of difference from the competition.

3 Thirty minutes in the manager's office to review the employee's employment packet containing the employee handbook, the promises and expectation page (see Rule 13) and maybe even a short discussion of the company's mission statement and operating principles.

4 In the last ten minutes of the new employee's shift, the department manager should escort the employee to the store manager's office for a short debriefing about the events of the first day (see Rule 14).

EMPLOYEE RETENTION RULES!

Often, the stress of the first day on the job can be overwhelming to a new employee, especially if it is his very first job. Sometimes a new employee decides not to return for the second day.

Many employers think someone who quits within the first few days is at fault. But I think it is more likely that the employee has been scared off. Retail is not easy, and many managers fail to realize how tough the first few days on a new job can be.

Think of a newbie as an infant or toddler who needs a lot of attention early on. Invest 72 minutes on Day One. Your efforts will pay off later as your new employee gets more comfortable and confident in the job.

Display a welcome poster.

EMPLOYEE RETENTION RULES!

Give new employees a hearty welcome. Start with a welcome poster so all the employees can get to know the new person quickly.

After the candidate has accepted your offer of employment, ask her to write a short (50 to 100 words) bio about herself. Be sure the new employee knows you want to use the information to help her get acquainted with other employees right away.

Take her photo, too and let her know that you are creating a welcome poster. Your local drug store (or even your own store) can develop the photo within hours.

You'll use the bio and photo to create a poster to display in the break room during the new hire's first four weeks. Headline the poster something like: "Welcome to the Team" or "New and Improved" (as in the *employee* is new and the *store* is improved because of her addition to the staff). Hang the poster on the bulletin board or near the time clock.

This simple announcement will impress your new employee because it shows you were prepared for her arrival. The poster took some planning. It also indicates that you are proud of the new employee. It's an internal "news release" for everyone to read.

Welcome to the company!

"Hello! My name is _____."

It has been said that the sweetest sound to most people is the sound of their own name. Let's make it easy for everyone to see and use co-workers' names.

I designed a special name badge for my restaurant's new hires. The badge was 2-1/2 inches round and red. It had a window for the employee's name, which was clearly visible from 20 feet away. This badge was different from the rectangular white name badge employees wore after their first month on the job.

The special badge for new employees helped everyone the employee came in contact with. When customers saw that the employee was new, they were more understanding of a slower pace or a small error. Co-workers learned each other's names quickly, and more experienced employees were eager to help the new ones—they remembered when they were new.

But the red name badge was a big help to me, too. It worked like a cue card for me to greet the newbie by name. Then I could introduce myself and thank him for joining our organization. It was great personal recognition for a new employee.

Give new employees a tour of the store.

Make your new hire feel right at home on the first day with a store tour. Here's what makes a good tour:

1   The store manager should conduct the tour with one, two, or three new employees—keep the group small.

2   The tour should take 20 to 30 minutes.

3   Start outside. Show employees where to

park. Explain that it's part of their job to look for any issues outside when they arrive at the store. Ask them to point out any problems they may see to their manager.

4   As you are walking through the store, introduce the new employees to as many co-workers as possible. The familiarity gained here will help build in-store relationships right away.

5   Point out the store's strategic points of difference to help the newbies become proud of the store. The fact you sell only USDA Choice Beef, have the market's largest salad bar, the most delicious store-made chicken salad, or the fastest checkout service is important for the new hires to know. Encourage the newbies to promote these features to customers.

White-collar employees are typically given a tour of the office on their first day. I think all employees deserve to see their new surroundings and meet their family of co-workers on Day One.

RULE
13

Promise a lot and expect a lot.

Good employees have many employment options. We are no longer in the days when applicants were plentiful and employees were grateful for any job. Since the pendulum has definitely swung in the employee's favor, we must do a far better job convincing candidates that we have a lot to offer.

Give each new employee a Promises/Expectations sheet. Have the store manager explain these Expectations and Promises on the first day (Rule 9). On one side of the sheet are the store's Top 10 Expectations for the new employee. Here's an idea of a few expectations you can list:

Please:

1 Arrive on time (five minutes before scheduled start).

2 Call at least one hour before your scheduled start if you are going to be late or absent.

3 Follow all handbook rules.

4 Escort customers to the item requested.

On the reverse side of the Promises/Expectations sheet are the Top 10 Promises to the employee. Here are a few suggestions for your list:

We promise:

1 Your work schedule will be posted by noon on Wednesday the week prior.

2 Your paycheck will be deposited by 5:00 p.m. on Thursday the week after you work.

3 You will be offered cross-training opportunities after your first six months.

4 A manager will always use "please" and "thank you" when you are asked to do something.

Any retailer will find it easy to identify ten promises and ten expectations for new employees. Being clear about what you will guarantee and what is expected of each employee is a professional way to start a working relationship.

End Day One with a conversation.

"Wow, I'm glad that's over!"

It's 9:00 p.m. and Brandon, an 18-year-old, just finished his first shift as a new supermarket clerk, hired to pack bags and carry out groceries. He had a rough day. After listening to two very unreasonable customers complaining about where the store had moved the teabags, cleaning up a gallon of vinegar someone dropped on the floor, and bringing in shopping carts from the snowy parking lot every hour, he found himself asking, "Why did I want this job?"

If you want to be sure your new employee will come back to work after the first day, find out how that day went. No new employee should ever be allowed to leave his first shift without a ten-minute debriefing with the most senior store manager on duty.

Start the conversation with these two questions:

1 "How did it go for you today?" Pay close attention to his facial reaction, not just what he says.

2 "What is the one thing about the job today that surprised you the most?" Note if the answer is positive ("You're certainly never bored") or negative ("I never knew customers could be so nasty").

If the newbie sounds more negative than positive, continue the conversation. Try to allay his concerns and commiserate with his frustrations. Explain that it does get better and that the first few days of any job are tough.

A short conversation at the end of an employee's first day can set a positive tone for all the days to follow.

Assign a buddy.

Remember that social gathering you walked into not knowing a soul? How uncomfortable did you feel? A new hire entering the store on the first day feels that way, too. Awkward and alone. Compound that feeling with an honest mistake or two or an unkind customer, and she'll have reasons enough to decide the job isn't worth having.

Assign a buddy to help the new employee. Make sure the buddy is an experienced employee who is respected by management and associates alike, and who can be a role model. Have the buddy accompany the new employee on as many breaks and lunches as their schedules will allow in the first month.

In larger operations, a new employee could have both a social buddy and a technical buddy. The technical buddy can help on the more specialized aspects of the job, especially when the department manager is not available.

Encourage your experienced employees to volunteer to be a buddy by compensating them for the additional responsibility. A permanent 25¢ to 50¢ per hour raise might be appropriate. Being a buddy can also be a precursor to further promotions. After a buddy has taught new employees the store's policies and procedures for a while, he has developed many useful skills.

A well-administered buddy program can get new recruits on board faster and with more confidence. Higher retention rates will result.

Connect with the family.

If you hire a lot of young people at entry-level jobs, it makes sense to involve the family of the employee. At that age, a young person probably still lives at home and her family will want to help the new employee be successful.

Start connecting with the employee's family right away. Send a welcome letter to your new teenage employee's parents to explain the company's mission and priorities. In the welcome letter, make it clear to parents that their child's health and education comes first—*before* the needs of the store. Invite the parents to visit during their child's first week of work to meet the store manager and see where their child will be working. Even if the parents decline the offer, the gesture is sure to be appreciated.

A great way to make a positive connection with a new employee's family is to give the new employee her first two-week schedule in advance. This gives the family time to plan how their family member (your new employee) will get to and from work every day. (Note: This two-week advance schedule is feasible because the new employee should only be having orientation and training activities during this time, which you can easily schedule ahead.)

With the family on board, both employee and parental loyalty for your store will grow.

Introduce new employees to the management team.

At some point in a new employee's first two weeks of employment, the department manager should bring him to the weekly department managers' meeting for a formal introduction. During the meeting, ask the employee to introduce himself and offer his first impressions of the store. A new employee's fresh perspective can shed light on ways to improve store operations or the orientation process.

Your new employee will no doubt be nervous to meet with the whole management staff, so give her a heads-up. Let her know the day before that she'll be attending the meeting and tell her you'll be asking for her initial opinion about the store. If you handle it right, a new employee will look favorably at the opportunity to meet the store management and offer her ideas.

It's another way for your company to show that you treat all employees professionally. It also subtly suggests to new employees that your company offers opportunities for future advancement.

Don't forget the goody bag!

Remember the goody bag you used to get at birthday parties? It was exciting—a special gift for you to bring home. Here's a way to make your orientation period more fun: give a "goody bag" to every new associate after his first three weeks.

At our store, we put six of our signature items in the goody bag, including a loaf of our own Italian bread, a pound of fresh ground beef, and some of our store-made macaroni salad.

There's an additional benefit to giving out this

kind of goody bag. You want your new associates to know about your signature items and endorse them to customers while on the job. When they get the goody bag, they'll try those items at home and enthusiastically tell customers about the ones they enjoyed.

Why offer the goody bag after the third week? It's part of the series of fun surprises you offer in the first 30 days on the job. You'll present the paycheck in person at the end of week two (Rule 23), give the goody bag after week three, and present the permanent name tag at the end of week four (Rule 20). When the orientation feels like a party, everyone has more fun!

Give employees the tools.

During an employee meeting in one of my restaurants, I asked my favorite question, "What's one thing you think is really stupid around here?" A cook, with fire in his eyes, said, "Trying to serve our customers on a busy Friday night without two fryers." That was the first time I learned that one of our fryers worked only half the time. The manager was reluctant to turn in a request to replace this $4,000 piece of equipment. I understood their frustration, and with Fourth of July weekend only five days away, I had a new fryer shipped priority from halfway across the country so as not to have a mutiny.

It's impossible to do a good job without having the right tools. Trying to serve customers while nursing finicky slicers, tired scanners, and worn-out brooms and mops is challenging. And employees tell me in focus group sessions that if management doesn't care that their equipment doesn't work, why should they? They think about leaving for a company "where management cares more."

Employees expect to have proper, working equipment to do the job. When you don't have the tools, employees leave.

If you are not financially able to make all the necessary equipment upgrades, create a priority list for capital expenditures by store. Update this list quarterly and include all planned purchases and repairs for at least the next twelve months. Share this list with your employees so they know that their tools are scheduled for replacement or repair.

P.S. My son Alex worked as a bouncer while attending the University of Virginia. Each night the closers would fight for the one and only dustpan in the entire bar, which they all needed to finish out their shifts. Employees would literally pay each other to get the lone dustpan first so they could clean their sections and get home!

Make your name badge special.

Remember the round temporary name badges you gave every new employee on Day One (Rule 11)? Trade them in during a special event that's just for new hires from the previous month. At the event, give them a big dose of company recognition. The employees should meet and greet the company's owner, president, or the store manager (whatever works best for your company). Use the event as an opportunity to give employees new information about your company. For example, have a Human

EMPLOYEE RETENTION RULES!

Resources representative explain key company policies, have the loss prevention manager explain how employees can help reduce store shrink, and so on.

The most important part of this event should be the ceremonious exchange of the temporary name badge for the permanent badge. This "official" name badge acts as a diploma—proof that the new employee has gotten to the next level. Make it really special by having the highest-ranking person at the event hand out the badge with a warm "Congratulations."

There are many ways to make a name badge special. Some retailers include the employee's hometown, high school, or years of service on the badge. I've seen badges that have a small line at the bottom: "Ask me about . . ." and in bold letters a subject the employee enjoys sharing with customers, such as "Scrapbooking," "Fly fishing," or "My love of chocolate." These are great conversation starters to help employees feel comfortable with both customers and fellow employees.

Everyone's name is special, and when you make the awarding of the name badge into a special event, you're saying to your month-old employees: "We're glad you're here and we want you to stay."

Invest 40 hours.

EMPLOYEE RETENTION RULES!

It takes twelve years in school to earn a high school diploma. Four more for a Bachelor's degree. How long does it take to "graduate" a new employee—an employee good enough to be left alone in a department on any given shift and be able to do a good job?

The average retailer gives a new employee only eight hours of orientation. Eight hours! Sounds absurd, doesn't it? There's so much to learn. So many potential mistakes that might not only disappoint a customer but seriously hurt the company through a food safety breach or a loss of property or assets.

Computer-based training classes, live observations, intensive shadowing, testing, scavenger hunts, lectures, and buddy interaction take hours. I recommend you allocate 40 hours for new employee orientation to prepare them for the long term. Wegmans, Starbucks, and Nugget Markets do.

Rushing employees through the training process is counterproductive and opens the door to employees' early exits. They will leave you for a competitor willing to make the upfront investment in the employee's long-term future.

Stop putting new employees on probation!

Can we stop referring to the employee's first 30 days on the job as the "Probationary Period"?

The term is negative, off-putting, and even intimidating.

Definition #1: "A trial period in which a student is given time to try to redeem failing grades or bad conduct."

Definition #2: "A criminal sentence consisting of a term of imprisonment that is suspended provided certain terms and conditions are met."

How do you think this sounds to a new

employee? Let's be more creative and positive. Call it an Orientation Period, Introductory Period, Welcome Week, or even "Let's Get Acquainted Month"!

In the first few weeks of any relationship, you want to put your best foot forward. Start with a welcoming term that says, "We're happy you're with us and we'll do what it takes to help you get off to a positive start in your new job."

PART THREE

Communication

Personally deliver the first paycheck.

The first paycheck an employee receives should be hand-delivered to the employee by the store manager. If their days off conflict, make the necessary plans for the exchange to take place.

> *"Julie, I wanted to personally pres-*
> *ent you with your first paycheck. We hope*
> *this will be the first of many to come. All*

employers have to give you one of these. But I hope you'll soon realize that we offer much more than just a paycheck. We want to create a meaningful employment relationship with you that will last for years."

Wow! That's a powerful message to a new employee!

If time permits, the store manager could continue the conversation and conduct a progress report with the new associate, similar to the one conducted during last ten minutes of the first day (Rule 14). The added attention will make the new associate feel important, and it will offer another opportunity to express concerns and ask questions. Communication of this kind is vital in the early stages of the employment relationship.

If you offer it, start direct deposit *after* the first paycheck is personally handed to the employee. It will be a sincere, meaningful, relationship-building experience.

Assign to-do lists.

The most-cited reasons why employees leave their jobs include boredom, lack of purpose, and an absence of clear direction. To help keep employees from leaving you, try this idea that addresses all three of these concerns: create to-do lists for your employees every day.

Give each employee a daily to-do list. The department manager writes the to-do lists and the store manager supervises to make sure the assignments are clear and achievable. Create separate lists for day and

evening shift employees. Give each assignment to one or more employees *by name*. Attach an estimated time to complete (ETC) to each task. When names and times are attached to an assignment, accountability and productivity improve.

Create the individual to-do lists in a way that requires the entire team to complete all the assignments. Then make sure everyone has access to the whole list. Post the to-do lists for everyone to see. At the end of the shift, the to-do list should be reviewed by the department or store manager and filed for use in preparing performance reviews.

A regular to-do list of job responsibilities gives employees direction, creates accountability, and fosters both verbal and written communication.

Post schedules sooner.

Most employees hate a variable work schedule—one that changes from week to week. Managing your personal life is tricky enough, but it's even harder when there's little to no advance knowledge of next week's work schedule.

Managers make it really difficult when they post associates' work schedules for the coming week on Friday or Saturday. How can anyone make plans with less than two days notice? It's almost impossible to coordinate the demands of school, doctor visits, second jobs, sports, and errands in so little time.

I recommend that managers post employees' weekly schedules (Sunday through Saturday) no later than the Wednesday before at 5:00 p.m.

Give your associates the ability to properly manage their lives. If your job schedule is tough for an employee to juggle, she is likely to become another turnover statistic.

Conduct one one-on-one a day.

Communication needs to continue beyond the employee's first 30 days. A great idea from the restaurant industry is to do "one-on-ones." Make time to take one employee aside every day for a ten-minute conversation about the employee's life both on the job and off.

In this brief conversation, the manager can show that she cares about the employee as a person, not just as a worker. Try a few questions such as: "What is the most challenging aspect of your job?" or "What is your favorite activity to do when you're not at work?" For employees who don't have many adults who listen, you may be providing a much-needed sounding board.

"Check your problems at the door when you come to work!" is an antiquated and counterproductive mindset. A one-on-one conversation between employee and manager demonstrates a sincere, caring workplace. It's a great way to show that you are there for all your associates.

RULE
27

Huddle twice a day.

A store huddle is a daily opportunity to bring together all departments to plan how to make the day (or evening) better for the store team and the customer. At around 8:00 a.m. each day, sound a signal over the intercom to cue each department to send a representative to the ten-minute huddle near the front center of the store.

Each employee who participates in the huddle brings anything newsworthy to share: a new product, new employee, problem with equipment, food demonstration item, need for assistance in building a lobby display—whatever. Each person has only one minute to educate, enlighten, or inform.

The sound of a timer after ten minutes brings the huddle to an end. Strict adherence to ten minutes will keep the sessions going every day because they only take ten minutes. Any longer and department managers may gripe. After all, they need to get their departments set up.

Try a second huddle sometime between 4:00 and 5:00 p.m. for the evening shift. Every retailer I know admits their evening performance is less than their level of execution during the day. Improve communication with an evening huddle to share the daytime information (i.e., we're out of the sugar that's on sale) with the people holding down the fort at night.

Better customer relations and more engaged employees are the short-term benefits of daily huddles. Done consistently, huddles are another tool that prove to employees that management is listening. Huddles keep the communication flowing within your store, which ultimately leads to more satisfied employees.

Hold TEAM meetings.

Employees want to know that their ideas and concerns are listened to, considered, and valued. That's an important part of retaining your best employees. To facilitate the flow of communication from the bottom up, hold monthly or quarterly TEAM meetings.

"TEAM" stands for Thoughts Exchanged between Associates and Management. The leader of

the meeting is no less than a store manager, but preferably a district supervisor or, in smaller companies, the president.

In my career in both the supermarket and restaurant industries, I looked forward to my monthly TEAM meetings. They allowed me to hear employee-related issues directly from the horse's mouth. Once I heard about them, I could deal with issues before they exploded into more serious problems. I was able to refine policies in our handbook, improve customer relations, and explain any employee or management terminations if a question was raised.

Our TEAM meetings evolved into a wonderful exchange of ideas on how to make our business better. For example, my property was Virginia Beach's first restaurant to go smoke-free. We did that after a TEAM meeting when an 18-year-old server asked, "Why do we allow smoking when our mission statement includes the words, 'in an unquestionably clean and safe restaurant'?" She was right—smoking, although legal in restaurants at the time, didn't match our mission. Because of her question in a TEAM meeting, we eliminated the smoking section from our restaurant.

TEAM meetings let you to put your ear to the ground on a regular basis so you can hear what's coming and take action.

Post positively.

Keep the work environment positive. When a store is punctuated with dozens of signs warning or threatening or written with condescending words, the work environment will have a negative atmosphere.

"Don't block this door!"

"You must have a receipt before consuming anything in the break room."

"No parking in the fire lane."

"This register is closed."

"Out of order!"

"No refunds without receipt."

"Do not enter!"

"Employees only."

Walk around your store and count the signs that send an unintentional but distinctly negative message. Think of ways to reword the same sign and give it a more positive tone. Some ideas:

> *Please, for safety reasons and because the Fire Marshal asked, do not block this door. Thank you.*

> _____
> *Manager's Name*

> *Sorry, this _____ is out of order. It will be repaired by ___(date)_____. Thank you for your patience.*

> _____
> *Manager's Name*

Creating a positive and motivating work environment takes time, a caring attitude, and open eyes to see what we are taping to our walls. Negative, disrespectful, and condescending messages can be transformed easily into instructional, informational, and polite reminders.

P.S. When you do post a message, sign it. With a bold marker. Avoid the ubiquitous ending . . . "Management." It's impersonal and obscure. If it's a worthy notice, sign your name at the end—preceded by a bold "Thank you."

Keep them in the loop.

High on the list of what employees want from a job is "the feeling of being in on things." Sure, employees care about salary, hours, and their job duties, but many think that knowing what is going on in the company is the number one consideration.

Give your employees information about your company. And do it before they read about it in the local newspaper.

Once a year, write a letter that summarizes the company's achievements in the past year. Give a brief outline of the company's goals for the new year. In my company, it was called the "State of the Company" letter. It also noted special achievements, both company and individual. I kept it conversational and low-key, and focused on the positive. The main purpose of the letter was to educate each employee (as well as their family members who read it) on the condition and direction of the company.

If you can, write a second letter six months after the first, with a more specific theme. You could give details on the retirement of a long-time employee or explain a new government regulation that is important for everyone to understand (i.e., a minimum wage increase).

I recommend sending these letters to employees' homes rather than handing them out at work. Two reasons for this: One, it feels more professional to receive this kind of company communication in a formal way. Two, family members at home are likely to read the letter if it is sent home, and you'll get even more family buy-in to your company.

Let your employees know what's happening. They'll feel empowered and valued when they know the inner workings of the company.

**Take it
from Abe!**

One of the best supermarket retailers in the United States is Publix. I had the privilege of spending some quality time with one of their top store managers, Abe. Two of the most impressive items Abe pointed out in his store were the door to his office and a poster in the break room.

Abe had physically removed the automatic closing mechanism on the door to his office door. He didn't like the symbolism of a constantly closed office door. If he needed the door closed, he would close it. Abe's open door policy made a big impression on employees.

Then Abe showed me a big, bold poster in the break room. It invited any employee who had a complaint or an idea to improve the store or company to complete an attached form and submit it to management. A company response was guaranteed within 30 days.

Associates need to receive feedback on their questions, complaints, and ideas. But store managers aren't able to respond to everything. Allowing the associates to take it to the next level is empowering. To be effective, organizational communication must be top down *and* bottom up. Publix gets it. They know how valuable insight offered by their people "in the trenches" can be.

Take it from Abe—an open door tells people you are available to them. And a poster that encourages people to make suggestions shows them you respect their opinions.

Be open about your pay scale.

Here's something else I saw in at the
break room at Publix: the entire pay
scale for every position was posted for everyone to see! In 30
years of consulting, I had
never seen this before.
Most companies try
to keep pay scales
a secret. In fact, in
some companies,
it's a terminable
offense to discuss
pay rates.

Why be hush-hush when it comes to the most basic components of an employment relationship? Let's hope you're not embarrassed by your low pay rates . . . or that you give more to favorites and less to everyone else and are afraid someone will find out.

There is no legitimate reason to keep pay scales a secret. Employees expect and deserve a level playing field. Any other alternative is simply unacceptable.

It's important to note that you don't have to be the best paying company in the area to post your pay scales. But you need to know what the competition is offering. If you are below others in your market, be ready to explain what else you offer that makes up the difference. If you don't have other redeeming employment benefits, adjust your pay scales or be prepared for employees to leave your company with regularity.

Give 'em the FAQs!

Customers have a lot of questions. Often, they are simple ones, like "Are you open this coming holiday?" or "Where is the rest room?" They want the facts.

So make sure your employees know the FAQs— the answers to customers' most frequently asked questions.

Create a list of the ten most frequently asked questions, along with short scripted answers. Many will be the same for any department: "What time do you close?" Others are

department specific: "Are the cakes made fresh here or were they frozen?" Give every employee this FAQ list during orientation and whenever employees cross-train in another department.

Here's how to create your FAQs: Ask each department manager to brainstorm with their employees the top ten questions asked by customers. Within a month each department should create the list of questions and submit it to the store manager. After each list is approved, give the department manager an additional month to answer each question simply but thoroughly. Then you'll have your FAQs list for every department in the store.

Employees want to be able to answer customers' questions. They do not like looking stupid. Armed with the answers to the most frequently asked questions, a new associate will feel empowered and more confident. In addition, you'll be building more superior customer relations when everyone has the FAQs.

Manage your store's
bulletin board.

I've seen too many store bulletin boards that are managed like bad break rooms . . . haphazardly. There are government-mandated posters, four-year-old company policy announcements, and yellowed notices from the head office. After a few years of mismanagement, the standard bulletin board becomes either an eyesore or like nondescript wallpaper.

But your bulletin board should be a great employee communication tool. Try this: use a bulletin board with three sections—two corkboard sections and one dry-erase section. (Even better, use three boards, each three by five feet—find the wall space!)

Display all government-mandated posters and information on one corkboard section. Showcase your company policies, announcements, and work schedules on the second corkboard section. Most employees will only refer to the board for the work schedules, but the rest of the information will be available if someone needs it.

Reserve the dry-erase section of the board for store management to write news and notes from yesterday, today, or tomorrow—*only*. Keep the board current, interesting, and ever-changing. Your associates will quickly get into the habit of checking that section of the bulletin board before starting their shift.

What kind of information is newsworthy? Well, as a start, employee birthdays, anniversaries, promotions, dean's list achievers, new items, sales promotions. Post information about new employees here, too. Make it about 25 percent company-related news and 75 percent employee information.

Write everything with colorful markers. And don't forget to show that the board's news is up-to-date by having the manager who writes the news initial and date it.

Employee retention is bolstered by a strong exchange of information. A well-managed bulletin board, looked after daily, is a very effective communication tool.

Give employees STLFT!

A great way to create a motivating work environment and build sales is to give your employees Something To Look Forward To (STLFT). People hate to be bored. Week after week of doing the same job can be debilitating.

I've always loved the excitement a storewide promotion generates. Eventually, I noticed the STLFT phenomenon happening. Employees were getting excited two or three weeks before the promotion, such as a barbeque in the parking lot to promote some specialty products. And for two or three weeks

STALE BREAD DAY

afterward, they would "buzz" about the fun event.

That gave me the idea of creating a calendar of events, spaced 30 days apart, to keep up enthusiasm throughout the year. As the excitement from the last event would begin to subside, the anticipation for the next would begin to bubble up.

While we know that the purpose of promotions is to increase sales, they have the additional and profound effect of stimulating employee interest and engagement. By strategically spacing events throughout the year, employees enjoy the exciting work environment. Everyone needs something to look forward to!

Sign 'em up!

Employees derive a great deal of job satisfaction from being involved. Rather than feeling the work is burdensome, you'll be surprised how often employees are eager to be part of a committee where they can contribute their ideas.

Set up a number of formal and informal store groups, committees, and task forces that meet throughout the year. Invite associates who have been with you for at least one year to join one (or more) of these groups. Such social and operational committees might include:

- Safety Committee

- Holiday Party Committee

- Shrink Task Force

- Kid's Club

- "Best Place to Work" Committee

- Community Fund-Raiser

- Store Decoration Committee

- Employee Recognition Team

These kinds of groups could meet monthly, quarterly, or annually, depending on the store's needs. Some may be created for a one-time event (i.e., a 50th anniversary celebration).

When employees are members of an organized group, they feel more involved and motivated to contribute to the team. Most people enjoy this kind of workplace participation. And this benefit is in addition to all the good the committee or task force was originally formed to achieve.

Be gracious about vacations.

Every company has vacation policies that allow employees to take time off after working some significant period of time—sometimes after six months, or usually, a whole year. When employees take their vacation time, make sure everyone is wishing them "bon voyage," not teasing them with these kinds of comments:

"Time off? When do you work?"

"You're off so much, you're making it easy for us to get used to doing the job without you."

"It must be nice . . . I wish I could go on vacation!"

"Another vacation? Already?"

Remember, employees who are able to take vacation time are not no-shows, short-timers, or below-average performers. They are your most loyal and dedicated staff members. They have been with you the longest to earn these vacation benefits. They are people who show up every day, year after year.

And what do they get in return? Teasing, sarcasm, and jokes that call into question their loyalty and work ethic, just for using a company benefit that is offered to everyone—earned time off.

Whenever I hear such remarks, I shut down any further conversation, apologize to the recipient, and verbally discipline the source in private right away. Employees won't feel appreciated when they are belittled for redeeming an earned company benefit.

Change your culture—celebrate upcoming vacations and thank long-time employees who have earned their time off.

Listen carefully.
Your employees are talking.

Employees do talk. But companies don't always listen. Slowdowns, work stoppages, and the formation of third-party unions are the result of management's proverbial deaf ear.

Today, most managers learn about their employees' level of engagement through the administration of regular employee attitude surveys (sometimes called culture surveys). Such surveys elicit honest feedback from all associates, including lower management.

In 2016, along with the Retail Feedback Group and the Food Marketing Institute, I conducted the first-ever food industry-wide department managers' attitude survey. The results were eye-opening and explained why retention rates for some key department manager positions are so poor.

Conduct an employee survey to identify any issues that are causing general discontent, early terminations, and ultimately lower retention rates. Once the survey is complete, a committee of managers and employees should meet to review the results and recommend appropriate actions.

Post the top five survey revelations on your employee bulletin board along with an action plan to address each issue. After each one is handled, cross the item off the posted list. That way, all employees will see a connection between employees speaking up and management taking action. That's empowering! An employee described this process: "We speak, they listen and act. This company cares."

Employees do talk. Be the one they talk to. Listen carefully and then act.

Build your company culture.

Business guru Peter Drucker is credited with this quote: "Culture eats strategy for breakfast." It applies directly to employee retention.

Management can focus enormous amounts of energy and time on creating the perfect business strategy, only to see it fail from a lack of execution because of a poor store culture. When a store culture has been neglected, you'll find too many employees who feel they don't really matter to management. That leads to lots of turnover and even to business failure.

A company's culture is paramount. It is the combination of a company's vision, mission statement, and values all multiplied by leadership's passion. A company's culture is at the foundation of everything the company undertakes. It can't be assumed or taken for granted, and it can't be bought.

When I purchased the franchise rights to develop a family restaurant company, I was purchasing recipes, procedures, systems, and blueprints. The company's culture was not included in the purchase price. I had to build it starting on day one and work at it every day of our existence. Unfortunately, a store's culture is not everlasting. A bad hire, an ill-conceived company policy, or an inept manager can erode a positive company culture.

Decide what you want your company to stand for and how every employee will contribute to that culture. Then work arduously every day to build it.

PART FOUR

Recognition

Recognize your best employees.

Mary Kay Ash, founder of Mary Kay Cosmetics, said, "People work for money but they live for praise and recognition." So let's give them plenty of acknowledgment.

Meaningful recognition programs can be administered daily, weekly, monthly, and annually. Let's start with a simple way to remember to acknowledge good work every day: the Ten Penny

Policy. A store manager keeps ten pennies in one pocket. Throughout the day, the manager compliments at least ten employees, and every time he does it, he moves a penny from one pocket to another to keep score.

A weekly recognition program can be goal related (highest sales, gross margin, etc.). After achieving a weekly milestone, a specific department or person can be recognized on the bulletin board, intercom, or Intranet.

Many companies offer monthly recognition through an Employee of the Month award. Don't use this program if it is no more than a popularity contest or if you award it to everyone over time so as to not hurt anyone's feelings. The award should be based on an objective scoring system and the same person (if that person is, in fact, the best) should be eligible to win it multiple times.

You can implement annual recognition programs based on birthdays, employment anniversaries, and performance reviews. These programs, done right, are fabulous motivators and everyone is a qualified potential recipient.

A paycheck is important, but I agree with Mary Kay: employees live for recognition.

Make your break room an oasis.

"Our company's greatest assets are our employees."

If that's true, your break room should be the best room in your building. The quality of the break room tells me how much management is committed to employees.

Your break room should be an oasis for your greatest assets to relax and recharge. Too often the location, design, and management of the break room are left to chance. It's typically like a big closet next to the receiving area that's outfitted with three milk crates (as chairs), a broken coffee pot, and two old magazines on a dilapidated table.

Go in your break room and sit down. Look around. Are you proud of what you see or does it look like an expanded janitor's closet? Would you be proud to bring some personal friends there to enjoy a beverage and some conversation? No? Then why are you offering such a place to your most valuable assets?

Some of the best break rooms I've seen include: pictures and bios of current managers that describe their career paths in the organization, posters of new employees (Rule 10), an updated daily bulletin board (Rule 34), a book exchange, free Wi-Fi, and a bowl of complimentary fresh fruit. One retailer I met puts free, freshly-made peanut butter and jelly sandwiches in the break room fridge so that no employee will ever go hungry. Wow! How is that for being employee-committed?

Invest in employee development.

I believe in the adage, "Give a man a fish and you'll feed him for a day, but teach a man to fish, and you'll feed him for a lifetime." Give employees a paycheck and you'll feed them for a week. Continuously "feed" them opportunities to do their job better and you'll give them career opportunities for a lifetime. Plus, you'll be encouraging them to stay with your company.

In my company, each manager had a $500 self-development fund. The company provided $500 per

year for managers to spend at their discretion on their own personal development. Options included taking a college class, attending a seminar, or going to an industry convention.

All employees need an opportunity to grow personally and professionally. Maybe a financial commitment of $500 per year makes sense for your managers; for lower-level employees, you could establish a 25¢ per hour accumulating development account that they can use when it reaches a substantial number. A non-financial commitment of a structured cross-training program (Rule 50) is another way to show your employees that your company is one that provides them with meaningful opportunities for a better future. And that's the kind of company employees want to stay with for the long run.

Display associates' photos and achievements.

Here's an easy and affordable way to give tangible recognition to employees' accomplishments: display employee photos and achievement certifications in each department.

Post photographs of the department manager and each employee in the department. Promote the "team" concept by giving the department a special name so employees feel part of the club—"The Deli Pros" or the "Fish Mongers."

Another way to recognize employees is to display their certifications. Becoming Food Safety Certified is a significant personal achievement. Display the certificates in the store. Employees will be proud and customers will be impressed.

After front-end employees complete their orientation training, make two professional-looking certificates. Give one to each new employee to take home, and post the other on the front wall of the store under a big headline: "We're Certified, We're Proud."

Other professions display their certifications (lawyers, pharmacists, fitness trainers, upscale car repair centers). They show other employees and customers that training and recognition is taken seriously. Try it in your store, too.

Make special events special.

Birthdays and employment anniversaries provide an opportunity for us to give our associates a dose of what they want—praise and recognition.

How many recognition programs does your company offer? And how much effort do you put into each one?

The variation of execution between companies is amazing. I know of one company that goes all out to celebrate an employee's birthday. The store manager sings "Happy Birthday" over the intercom as one person from each department converge on the birthday boy or girl with cake (fresh), cluster of balloons and a card signed by all. It's an impressive sight. Certainly high on the recognition scale. Another company puts one cake (beyond the sell-by date) on the break room table each Saturday morning. On top of the cake are the names of all employees who have a birthday that week. I asked the manager on duty what would happen if the birthday boy or girl didn't work on Saturday. The blank look on the manager's face gave me the answer I suspected.

To insure effective execution of all your recognition programs, create a recognition committee with three to five managers and senior employees whose job it is to see that all birthdays and work anniversaries are properly organized and enthusiastically executed. Avoid at all costs any appearance of favoritism.

All employees have birthdays and work anniversaries—two important, personal events each year when an employee can enjoy the spotlight. Don't lose this opportunity to make your employees feel special.

PART FIVE

Discipline

Hire slowly and terminate quickly.

Every company needs a consistent process for terminating employees. There should be a finite number of progressive steps to take before an employee is terminated.

Encourage managers to follow the company's discipline process carefully. Everyone in the store is depending on them to take corrective action when needed and rid the workplace of the occasional troublemaker in a timely manner.

When management is not swift to remove people who deserve to be fired, here's what happens:

- The very best employees leave. Winners don't want to be associated with losers.

- Average employees stop trying to become better. If underperformers aren't called out, why should they try to improve?

- Below average employees will feel even more comfortable to remain below average. After all, there don't seem to be any consequences.

Think of your favorite teacher or coach growing up. Most share the same characteristic: holding you more accountable and expecting more of you than anyone else did—and you measured up because they expected it!

Prune the grapevine.

As a rule, managers are taught not to share information about terminations. When a current employee inquires about an employee who has been fired, only vague, general statements are offered. Managers defend their terse explanations with the "need to know" argument: other employees don't need to know the details about why another employee has left.

I strongly disagree. Terminated employees, especially for serious cause, often don't tell the truth about why they were terminated. In fact, they tend to blame others, especially management, for treatment they saw as unfair. Current employees will talk with terminated employees and are likely to believe only the ex-employee's side of the story. By not defending yourself, you risk losing credibility and good faith with your employees.

Prune the grapevine—tell everything you legally are able to tell about controversial matters to the other employees so inaccurate gossip doesn't take hold of your workforce. Your employees need to hear management's side of the story. Not every detail, of course, but enough to explain away the untruths that may be spread by the terminated employee trying to save face or retaliate.

Nasty rumors destabilize and debilitate an organization. When someone tries to impugn your reputation you must defend yourself. Check with Human Resources, the company attorney, or whomever you need to give you advice about what you can say, but don't remain silent after a messy termination. The other side won't.

PART SIX

Evaluation

Don't call it a performance evaluation.

The term "performance evaluation" has negative connotations. No one enjoys being "evaluated." And who really wants to be an "evaluator?" Managers and employees alike begin to squirm when they hear the term.

A popular alternative, "performance review," is flawed, too. By definition, it is skewed toward past performance—it's a "review." Once the review form is completed and signed by both parties, the manager considers the job done. But where is the improvement plan for the employee to follow going forward?

Most managers haven't been trained on how to properly conduct a performance evaluation. They mimic what they experienced, perpetuating mistakes and poor practices. "Hear, read this, then sign it. It's your review." "Got a few minutes? I want to go over your evaluation. HR is on my back to get it done." Sound familiar?

I have a new name for the performance evaluation: the "success plan." When you sit down together to talk about planning for the employee' successful future, you're well on your way to retaining that employee.

Start by telling the employee a week ahead of time that you'll be talking about her success plan. Give her a chance to prepare for it. Listen to her concerns about the job. Set goals for the future.

For more ideas, check the Appendix, where I've listed ten rules to follow for an effective success plan.

Don't evaluate employees. Plan for their success!

Find the tick.

Story 1: An old man gets up from his easy chair to let his dog into the house. The dog sits down and proceeds to scratch incessantly. Annoyed, the old man gives the dog a kick to stop. The dog, now annoyed by both the itch and the kick, gets up and takes refuge in the far corner of the room to sit and continue scratching.

Story 2: An old man gets up from his easy chair to let his dog into the house. The dog sits down and proceeds to scratch incessantly. This man watches his

dog closely, then feels in his fur, finds, and removes a tick that was causing the itch. The man and his dog settle down in their respective spots for a little nap. The moral? Don't get annoyed or angry at a symptom of a problem. "Find the tick" and solve the problem.

I meet plenty of managers who complain about not being able to find and keep good help. They become frustrated by the constant turnover they experience in their store. Managers make these kinds of remarks: "These kids don't really want to work," and "Employees today don't have the work ethic they used to." But they have done little to analyze their real problems of hiring and retention.

Look for the ticks in your operations to figure out why you have employee issues. Analyze your applicant sources, evaluate your interview process, and look for weaknesses in your orientation program. Use exit interviews to learn why employees leave.

Find the tick (or ticks) that causes your turnover problems. That's how to solve those problems and improve employee retention.

Include turnover as part of managers' compensation.

Employee turnover is expensive. We noted in the Introduction that the cost of recruiting and training to replace an entry-level employee is, on average, $3,500. Studies have also found a correlation between a stable team of employees with low turnover and higher customer satisfaction.

Everyone measures store sales to maintain a laser-like focus on growing them. If you measure employee turnover as carefully and consistently as sales, you help management focus on improving employee retention. Measure your employee turnover by store every year.

Once turnover has been measured, take the extra step of using that metric as a partial basis for determining your managers' bonuses. Here's an idea: base 20 percent of a store manager's bonus on the results of the store's annual employee attitude survey and/or the store's employee retention statistics. Store managers who work hard to build strong employee retention rates and higher customer satisfaction scores deserve recognition and additional remuneration. Store success depends on much more than short-term gross margin or sales goals.

Reward your managers who understand the importance of low employee turnover and high retention rates.

Cross-train employees.

One of the most underutilized educational opportunities in the retail world is cross-training. This classic job enrichment opportunity is typically administered in emergency situations . . . like when Janice quits without notice.

"Who can work in the deli now that Janice has quit?"

"Well, Phil in grocery once said that he loved watching the deli slicers."

"Okay, let's give him a try."

We can do better. A structured cross-training program is an ideal way to offer growth opportunities

to your employees. Cross-training opportunities should be listed on your Top 10 Promises sheet (Rule 13) and promoted on your website where you offer employment opportunities.

A structured cross-training program requires some effort to administer. There's the application process, scheduling, and a training agenda the employee has to complete before being certified. I encourage retailers to add a colored star on the employee's name badge for each department the employee has been certified to work. It's empowering to the employee and a great way to recognize the achievement of being cross-trained.

A secondary benefit of a cross-training program is the flexibility it provides. Having several store employees cross-trained in multiple departments is a godsend for any store manager.

Make an effort to cross-train employees. It's a win-win for everyone!

Be a positive presence.

Too many company supervisors call on their stores like a stealth bomber. They swoop in without notice, drop their payload (nega-tive remarks), and leave behind frustrated managers, demoral-ized workers, and a reduced level of store morale.

A supervisor's role cannot be to simply point out problems with-out working with people to solve them. A supervi-sor is supposed to have "super vision." Shouldn't this super vision help them see that people don't respond well to a barrage of negativism?

At least fifty percent of a supervisor's visits should be announced, not a surprise. If the supervisor is truly the expert and the best technical resource the company has, then why shouldn't the visit be scheduled days in advance so the people in the store or department can be available to take advantage of the supervisor's expertise?

There is no question as to the benefit derived from calling on a store that is not expecting a visit from headquarters. But if all visits are unannounced, the important exchanges of information to aid the employees and department's growth and development might never take place. Even worse, you run the risk of creating a "them versus us" culture that doesn't foster employee retention.

Find out why they leave.

Don't ever let an employee leave the company without asking for the real reason for his/her departure.

Employees frequently say they're leaving for more money when there is almost always another reason. When employees do leave, it is typically to get away from something they can't stand any longer. Only when the job becomes downright unbearable do they quit.

You can do an exit interview face-to-face or in writing. I recommend doing the exit interview in writing (less pressure on the employee) and on the

day the employee picks up his last paycheck (the employee has had a week to cool off and is more rational). Make sure your exit interview form gives employees the chance to tell you honestly why they are leaving.

Analyzing an employee's departure is an opportunity for management to learn some lessons:

1 Did we hire the wrong person? In other words, did something go wrong in our selection process?

2 If it was the right person, did something go wrong during the orientation process that caused the departure?

3 If not those, what went wrong in the timeframe after orientation and before the employee quit?

An introspective assessment of the departure and the departing employee's responses to an exit interview should give management insight into what actually went wrong. You might find a reason that you can fix. I've read (and I believe it!) that management is to blame for 80 percent of all terminations. Find out why employees leave, so you can make the changes that will encourage future employees to stay.

Deliver more than employees expect.

I teach a seminar on achieving superior customer relations that includes this algebraic expression: $D>E$. It means if we deliver (D) more than (>) the customer expects (E), they'll be wowed. Escorting a customer to an item and offering her a carry basket, taking her grocery bags out to the car and offering her child a lollipop, or calling a customer two days after she purchased a big order for a party to make sure everything was just right—these can

wow a customer. And when you wow customers, they return.

Why not embrace the D>E concept to achieve superior *employee* relations? Deliver more than your employees expect on the job.

Exceed their expectations by greeting each one personally, holding an energizing afternoon huddle, or posting their names on top of a sales leader board. With every "wow!" their loyalty to your company will grow.

Offering minimum wage, minimum training, minimum recognition, and minimum opportunities will yield minimum loyalty. That's not algebra. That's common sense.

Deliver more to your employees than they expect. You'll find you're spending less time in your office plowing through job applications and more time building your successful business!

Ten Rules for a Successful Success Plan

1 **Give your employee one week to get ready.**
Give the employee at least one week's notice of the success plan meeting so he can prepare. Give the employee a success plan form to complete and submit to you a day or two before the actual review. You'll get an idea of how the employee sees his own performance, which will clue you to possible areas that will require additional thought and preparation on your end. If you find that the employee's ratings and your ratings are off by more than 20 percent (i.e., your score was 4 and the employee's score is 6 on a 1 - 10 scale), identify examples to support your score or be prepared to change it.

2 **Spend as much time preparing for the review as you spend conducting the review.**
A 60-minute success plan session will require 60 minutes of prep time. Review the employee's self-review, to talk to previous supervisors, review his current job description, peruse the employee's file, and create goals for the employee for the next twelve months.

3 **Make the meeting comfortable.**

Don't allow people to disturb you during the meeting. Have your calls held so you aren't interrupted. This shows your employee how serious you are about the meeting. Offer your employee coffee or water, as you would to another colleague in a meeting. Give enough time to get the job done. For part-time employees, a success plan meeting should take at least 30 minutes. For full-time employees, take 60 minutes, minimum. Plan on 90 minutes for a middle manager and two hours for top management. Don't look at your watch during the review process—better yet, stick it in your desk drawer. You want the employee to feel that you have time for the session and are giving it your complete attention.

4   Have two-to-one meetings.

Include three people at the success plan meeting: the employee, the reviewer, and the reviewer's immediate boss. It's a win, win, win situation. The employee gets to shine in front of two levels of management. The reviewer can demonstrate to her boss how well she develops staff members. And the big boss gets to conduct an informal personnel inventory to identify future stars or areas that need improvement. But be careful that your employee isn't intimidated by having two members of management at the meeting. Here's an idea— the reviewer sits on one side of the table and the employee and reviewer's boss sit on the other side. Positioning the big boss on the same side as the employee bolsters the employee's confidence.

5   Listen more than talk.

During the success plan meeting, management personnel should talk much less than the employee.

You're trying to hear how the employee feels about her job, what she hopes will be her career path, what works and doesn't work in her job responsibilities. You want the employee to command 70 percent of the conversation. The reviewer should talk no more than 25 percent of the time, and the senior manager should occupy only about 5 percent of the airtime. You'll learn much more by asking your employee questions that draw her out, and then really listening to her answers.

6 Be flexible.

During the success plan meeting, the reviewer should use the review form that the employee has already filled out before the meeting. Use another color pen during the meeting to make notes on the form during the meeting. While you're listening carefully (see previous rule), the employee might convince you to change a score or comment. Don't be afraid to alter your thinking when warranted. It shows that you listen, respect the employee's viewpoint, and have flexibility.

7 Avoid halos and sandwiches.

You want to be sure your reviews aren't skewed by the halo effect. That's when the reviewer has a personal bias toward one performance category and mentally directs all the other scores in that direction. For example, you might believe that customer service is the most important attribute for an employee to possess. As a result, you give higher scores on all criteria to an employee who is really good with customers. But you want to measure each category separate and apart from the others.

Another thing to avoid during a success plan meeting is "sandwiching" criticism between compliments. Don't say: "You're very personable with the guests, but your cash control is poor. But don't get me wrong, I'm glad you're so friendly." Instead of sneaking past poor performance, take time to discuss the problem and find ways to resolve it.

8 Give examples and comments.

Fill up all the space on the review form with comments, examples, elaborations, or clarifications. Review forms stay in the employee's file, and future managers will be able to use them. A score of "B" or a "3" mean nothing without supporting explanation. Clear, specific, and honest comments will build a better success plan process.

9 Separate the success plan meeting from the discussion of pay.

Although pay and performance are usually in lock step with one another, it's a good idea to separate the discussion on any associate's performance with the discussion on a pay adjustment by at least a month. When you end the performance review session with the amount of the pay raise, you'll find that employees aren't listening to anything before the "show me the money" statement. And in a case where an employee receives less than he had hoped for, you've lost all the positive energy that was generated in the meeting. When you separate the two discussions, the performance goals can be digested and work can begin on them before any discussion of pay arises.

10 End the meeting by setting goals.

Specific goals give employees a clear direction for improvement and growth with the company. Make the goals SMART: specific, measurable, actionable, realistic, and timed. Goals should address the employee's strengths and weaknesses.

Make sure you don't overload goals onto the employee—three to seven goals for next year are plenty. You can even add a personal goal into the mix. Try asking, "Do you have a personal goal that would you like to accomplish this year, and how can I help you achieve it?" You might help employees stop smoking, go back to school, read more, or even improve their golf game.

Spend more than half the meeting talking about goals for the future. That's the surest way to plan for success!

Two Notes from Harold

NOTE 1

At least three charities will benefit from your purchase of this book. The publisher and I worked hard to minimize the production costs. I pledge to contribute all proceeds (after costs of production are paid) to help children, help animals in need, and feed the hungry. Thanks for assisting us in this endeavor.

NOTE 2

I'd love to hear from you regarding which Rule(s) you liked the best or if you have another Rule to add. Please email me at harold@hlloydpresents.com. If your employee retention rate increases markedly because you've implemented some of these Rules, be sure to let me know!